The
GOLDEN
KEY
to
HAPPINESS

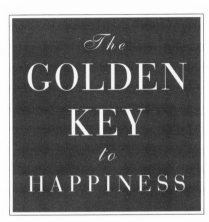

The GOLDEN KEY to HAPPINESS

Words of Guidance and Wisdom

MASAMI SAIONJI

Translated by Kyoko Selden
Edited by Elaine Hughes

ELEMENT
Shaftesbury, Dorset ◆ Rockport, Massachusetts
Brisbane, Queensland

Published in Great Britain in 1995 by
ELEMENT BOOKS LIMITED
Shaftesbury, Dorset SP7 8BP

Published in the USA in 1995 by
ELEMENT BOOKS, INC
PO Box 830, Rockport, MA 01966

Published in Australia in 1995 by
ELEMENT BOOKS LIMITED
for JACARANDA WILEY LIMITED
33 Park Road, Milton, Brisbane, 4064

Designed and Typeset by
BRIDGEWATER BOOKS

Printed and bound in Great Britain

British Library Cataloguing in Publication data available

Library of Congress Cataloging in Publication
Saionji, Masami

The golden key to happiness:
words of guidance and wisdom/Masami Saionji
p.cm.
Previously published:
NEW YORK: SOCIETY OF PRAYER FOR WORLD PEACE. c1990
Translated from the Japanese
1. HAPPINESS 2. PEACE OF MIND 3. TITLE
BJ1481. S28 1995
170'. 44–dc20

ISBN 1- 85230-711-0

A book of light and joy...

Although we try to turn our attention to the essence of life – the spiritual nature of human beings – nowadays we tend to be swayed by the objects and phenomena right before our eyes. The ring of truth that comes from *The Golden Key to Happiness* will touch hearts and this will become a book of light and joy for many people.

This is a must book for everyone who is training in AIKIDO. The founder of AIKIDO, Morihei Ueshiba, and the founder of the World Peace Prayer Society, Masahisa Goi, shared the same high ideals. Mrs Saionji, whose heart and spirit are one with Mr Goi, expresses the spirit of AIKIDO perfectly.

As people read this book of light, I pray that the spirit of peace may prevail throughout the world.

KISSHOMARU UESHIBA
Aikido Doshu

Words of guidance and wisdom...

At times, we need some guidance in our lives. When our daily lives are comfortable, smooth, and without any problems, we are very happy. However, most of us feel troubled, in pain, worried, frustrated or irritated during the course of each day. All of us have wondered, at some time or other, how wonderful it would be if we could live with hope and joy at all times. Some of us may have looked for guidance when troubled, hoping that it would heal our tired hearts and that it would guide us in the right direction.

This book is filled with wonderful words of guidance and wisdom. Mrs Masami Saionji has taught me the spirit of true peace over the years, during which time I have had the pleasure of knowing her personally. In this book, she shows us the most important points in life – such as living courageously and never giving up. I sincerely believe that this remarkable book will give true peace to the hearts of many people. I recommend it to anyone who wishes to attain true peace of mind.

SOSHITSU SEN xv
Grand Tea Master of Urasenke

CONTENTS

CONTENTS

INTRODUCTION

Do you know the primary cause of happiness and unhappiness in your only one and precious life? Your own mind creates the destiny of your life.

How, then, indeed, does your mind create happiness or unhappiness? By thinking.

God created all by thinking. Therefore we can also create everything, including our wonderful destinies, by thinking. God, nations, parents and nature do affect our destinies; but mainly it is our own will that creates our lives. What you envision in your mind is itself a strong power of creation, a power of manifestation, and a power of great value. If you wish to create a good destiny, you must think and project only good and positive thoughts at all times. Then you will be able to lead a happy life.

On the other hand, when you imagine misfortune, poor health or illness in your future and constantly worry about it, then negative things will manifest themselves in your world, just as you thought. The golden key to happiness is to always think positive thoughts, and never negative ones.

Everyone genuinely wishes to lead a happy life. But in order to lead a happy life, you must first know how to lead such a life. You will find such a way of life – the key to happiness – in this book. When your heart aches, when you are troubled or feel sad, open this book. Then you will find that your way of thinking is changing or your way of looking at the situation is changing. As a result, all your troubles will disappear. When your thinking changes, you will be able to start building a bright and luminous future with your own hand, with your own power. There is no need to despair, even if the situation or circumstances you are in may seem hopeless to you. Everyone, without exception, will find true peace in life by changing the old way of thinking into a positive, light-filled way of thinking and by envisioning good and wonderful things and a luminous future as much as possible.

Let us open the door to our hearts – the door that was hidden up till now. Fill the room behind the door with true, radiant and happy ways of living. When your heart is completely filled with light, positive thoughts, you will naturally be able to envision only good in your mind without any force or effort.

As you read this book, I sincerely hope you will start building your life toward a wonderful and luminous future from this day on.

MASAMI SAIONJI

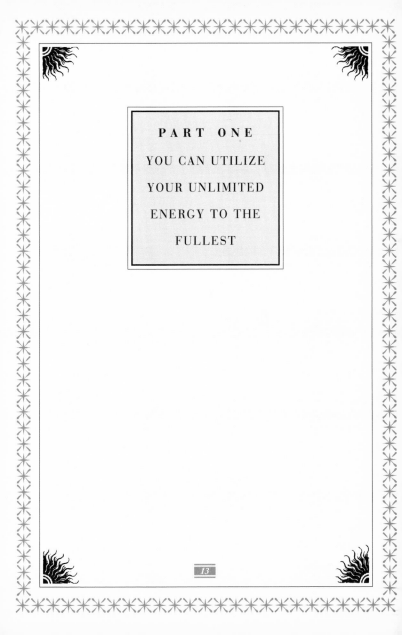

PART ONE

YOU CAN UTILIZE YOUR UNLIMITED ENERGY TO THE FULLEST

c h a p t e r

1

REALIZE YOUR
UNLIMITED POWER

The universe is filled with unlimited power. This same unlimited power is in all human beings. The purpose of life is to prove that unlimited power, unlimited love, unlimited wisdom, unlimited richness, unlimited potential, and unlimited health are inherent in the self by bringing them forth one by one and expressing them through your existence.

I would like to tell you: You have the power to overcome your problem no matter what happens. Use it. Go ahead and call forth that power. Try your best to do so. No matter how complex and difficult the problem may seem, it is really simple and easy if you go to its roots. There is nothing that cannot be solved. Your fear and insecurity only enlarge your problem.

Effort is the only effective way to draw forth the unlimited potential given equally to every human being. Through making efforts, human beings can claim the endless potential that is already given them. If you spend the whole day without making effort, your endless potential will sleep forever. It's crucial to wake as quickly as possible. Through your awakening, the environment in which you have lived will quickly be transformed, and a wonderful world will start being built around you.

'What is impossible today will be possible tomorrow – or I will make it possible.' This is what you should firmly repeat to yourself many times.

You must never forget that every human being has latent, unconquerable power to repel any circumstance, any fate. If you succumb to your environment and your fate, that'll be the end. Nothing new will be born from your state of resignation. Constantly revive your power to overturn unwanted circumstances.

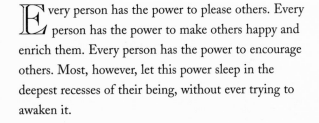

Every person has the power to please others. Every person has the power to make others happy and enrich them. Every person has the power to encourage others. Most, however, let this power sleep in the deepest recesses of their being, without ever trying to awaken it.

You must not let the power that you have sleep forever. In order not to let it sleep, purposely undertake a new challenge now. Lessons, sports, work – anything will do. Or strengthen your efforts in what you are already doing so that you can do much better than before. When you put this into practice, you'll be surprised to find that you still have abundant power in store. The more energy you use, the more energy will spring forth with overwhelming power.

When you have absolute faith in your hidden power, your talent will be demonstrated. The first step, when facing a job you have to do or a difficulty you have to solve, is to believe that you can definitely handle this task. Have total faith in your power. In this way you'll be able to accomplish any task, however difficult.

Everyone wishes for 'power'. But 'power' itself has no power. If good people possess power, the power becomes wonderfully strong. Such people demonstrate great power, leading the world to peace and others to happiness. However, if evil people possess power, the power demonstrates the violence called authority. Such people demonstrate their power in murders and war, leading people to darkness. That's the nature of power. Why do you think you need power? If you think you need power for the sake of achieving your selfish desires, you are better off without it. If you wish for power to lead mankind to peace, God will grant you that right now.

enerally, to change yourself, you need numerous experiences and an amazing amount of time. However, if only you will bring the great power of imagination and concentration into full play, you can change yourself in an instant. All you need to do is imagine your ideal image intensely, and pour your energy into it.

When you are standing at the limits of your ability, or when you are facing a crisis, do you know how to protect yourself? Miraculously, everybody knows how. If you have never been placed in such a situation, you may think you don't know how. But everyone is endowed with a skill to override crises. Even a newborn knows how to protect itself. How wonderful our adaptability is!

Let's imagine facing great difficulty, adversity, despair – the rock bottom. At first we will experience such pain that we may almost become insane, thinking we will never recover from the wound in our heart. However, the hidden power within begins to demonstrate great power beyond any human imagination. Gradually, power to adapt to the situation is born, and strength to persevere develops. Thus, all of us surmount a crisis by our own personal methods. This power is the latent ability given equally to everyone by God.

YOUR THOUGHTS
CREATE YOUR LIFE

The mind is energy, so it's possible to create everything using the mind as the motor. How does the mind enable you to create everything? By thinking.

When we see ourselves reflected in a mirror that illuminates the past, we find that the majority of us project evil, dark thoughts rather than good, bright thoughts. The same will be true if you just think back on your day. Many of you will certainly notice that between the time you awoke and the time you retired at night, you complained, and you criticized and badmouthed others more often than you praised them with cheerful words. Let's change that from today on.

Nothing is so scary as blind belief. Those who blindly believe that they are the most unhappy people in the world; those who believe that they are defeated no matter what they may do; those who believe that they are other people's laughing stocks; those who believe that they are no good, however hard they exert themselves or persevere – as long as they unwaveringly believe that they are unfortunate, they cannot exit from their misfortune. Unless they sever themselves from these kinds of blind belief, they can only be unhappy, for the universal law is that the world moves in accordance with one's thoughts. Nothing but your own blind belief in despair can create despair in this unlimited, wide world of the self.

If you wish to liberate the spiritual energy that resides in the heart and body, so that you can live in a free and joyous way at all times, you must reject thoughts that tie down your heart – such as dark depression, anger, fear, and anxiety. To let spiritual energy grow in your heart and let it manifest its power fully, you constantly need thoughts of gratitude, admiration, and cheerfulness.

Nothing in this world obstructs you. Your own thought that something obstructs you is the only thing that obstructs you.

Our consciousness, by its very nature, can control our physical functions, emotions, and thoughts, perfectly.

Your life takes shape this way: First, desire exists; it is gradually warmed in your heart; it grows and is born. It is not created by others' thoughts, by others' expectations, by others' way of life, or by others' power. Your true desire will always be fulfilled. Your essential wishes that spring from the bottom of your heart are the secret to accomplishing everything.

Determine in your heart what you wish to do, and advance straight toward your goal. Never let your heart stray from the goal that you genuinely want to reach. It's important to draw into your heart the goal you wish to achieve and keep it there for a long time. When the right time comes, that goal will definitely be fulfilled. Until one goal is achieved, don't think of unnecessary things. Don't let your heart wander elsewhere. Don't let others' opinions sway you. Concentrate on one goal with all your heart.

What you think about day and night forms your character and personality. When walking on the street, we sometimes encounter a person of striking spiritual beauty. It's as if the noble thoughts they think every day are spontaneously conveyed to us. The way you think determines exactly what you become.

It is your own attitude, or your own way of looking at things, that makes things worse or makes them appear worse. If you don't acknowledge the bad side of things, bad things don't even exist. Only divinity exists.

It's important to handle negative emotions within you as much as possible, trying not to express them. By negative emotions, I mean, for example, statements like 'No good', 'Can't do it', 'No!', 'Miserable', 'Stupid', 'Don't like', 'Want to die', and so forth. If these thoughts and emotions sneak into your mind and heart, try immediately to process them within you before you express them in word and attitude. Try always to dwell on positive emotions: 'I can certainly do it'; 'I like everyone'; 'I will be useful to others'; 'Everything will certainly improve'; 'It's all right'; 'I can overcome it'; 'I will never run away no matter what'; 'I will confront the situation.' If you keep having these positive thoughts all the time, miraculously you will be able naturally to do as your thoughts predicted.

'The glass is half empty' and 'The glass is half full.'

'I'm so old that I can't even do that kind of thing' and 'I'm not so old that I can't do that.'

'These are the last days of my remaining life' and 'Today is the first day of my remaining life.'

'There's no tomorrow' and 'There's always tomorrow.'

'I have only ten years left in my life' and 'I have as many as ten years ahead of me.'

'My legs don't move' and 'I can still use my hands.'

These two ways of expression refer to the same situations, yet they divide the world into light and dark, plus and minus, positive and negative.

Which way are you thinking every day? If your thinking is all dark and negative, your days must be melancholy and suffocating and your life hopeless. Change your way of thinking right away. Direct your thinking toward the positive way of life, toward the plus energy; then your life will definitely go upward.

If you always fear failure, you will definitely fail. If you constantly worry about illness, you will one day contract illness. If you always try to think about joyful, happy things, and behave as cheerfully as possible, you will certainly become happy some day.

Even if you succeed in running away from the circumstances given to you, the same circumstances will run after you, because your environment and circumstances do not change as long as your mind and heart do not change. The environment and circumstances given to you now constitute the world you have long depicted in your mind and heart; they represent an evolution of the world you have envisioned. People often think that other people and the society are to blame for every event that takes place around them, but that is not the case. Every event that evolves around you is made from the vibrations of your thought. If the vibrations of your thought are always wonderful and cheerful, your surroundings undoubtedly will make a world always filled with happiness and laughter. If the vibrations of your thought are gloomy and dank, the atmosphere that surrounds you will always be dark and unpleasant. The principle is not that you change when your surroundings change, but that your surroundings change when you change.

Sometimes one's thoughts race around endlessly, flying wildly as if they do not know how to stop. It's fine to race toward a bright, radiant future. However, it is not good to let your thoughts wander into the abyss of dark and lonely solitude, which, once you step in, may pull you down to the boundless world of darkness. At times your thoughts may bring back to this concrete world, unmodified, the events that happened in that dark world. When your mind wishes to leap toward the dark on its own accord, that's the exact moment you need to put the brakes on it.

One cannot possibly become unhappy if there is no doubt whatsoever in the mind. Your doubt destroys all the happiness in your life. Doubt falls into the mind the moment you distance yourself from the law of the universe, and doubt attracts negative thoughts. To give these negative thoughts no space to enter, you must always direct your mind toward God.

All of us are capable of following the way of life we have determined to follow.

All of us are capable of becoming as happy as we have determined to be.

All of us are capable of getting as much as we have determined to get.

All of us are capable of living as we have determined to live.

All of us are capable of maintaining as much health as we have determined to maintain.

In short, our lives unfold exactly the way we have wished and envisioned.

YOUR WORDS ARE ALIVE

Words have overwhelming power. If the same word is repeated over and over, a lie becomes the truth, and truth becomes a lie. Through repeating it many times, you gradually become that very word. Frequent repetition leads to self-hypnosis. If you fall into self-hypnosis through repetition of evil words, it will require considerable effort and perseverance to escape from it.

The energy of our every thought, action, or word, once it has been projected, lasts eternally without disappearing. This is the law of this world. Not only that, thoughts, actions, and words have the power to draw to themselves whatever elements are necessary to become concrete reality. Your own thoughts, actions, and words are all responsible for your fortune, whether good or bad.

Let's aim at the following at all times as we live our lives: Let us live this day to the fullest and speak only words of goodness, love, and care, refraining from any kind of evil words. If someone mouths evil words, let's have the good sense to change the topic instantly.

Don't be too greedy for your own good. If you have unconditionally taken in all the words that flood this world, you have acquired an enormous burden. You have lost your freedom; you are in pain; you are panting. How foolish and pitiful that is! If there were a system in this world for buying words, would you really buy all of them, unconditionally? I think not. You would think hard and evaluate them before you bought any. You would not have enough money or energy to buy all the words, nor would you have to buy words that would work against you, such as words you dislike or that displease you. Then what

kind of words would you buy most? You would shop
for words that encourage, enliven, or stimulate yourself
and others – happy, peaceful, or inspiring words.

Yes, that's fine. Pretend that you are buying words;
evaluate well and store carefully your chosen words
within yourself. Don't ever be greedy.

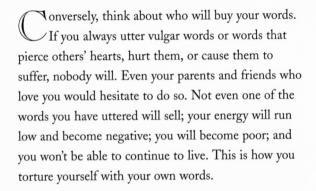

Conversely, think about who will buy your words.
If you always utter vulgar words or words that
pierce others' hearts, hurt them, or cause them to
suffer, nobody will. Even your parents and friends who
love you would hesitate to do so. Not even one of the
words you have uttered will sell; your energy will run
low and become negative; you will become poor; and
you won't be able to continue to live. This is how you
torture yourself with your own words.

Another thing. If you only keep buying words, even good ones, your money and your positive energy will decrease. You need to gain too, after all. If so, isn't it preferable to sell rather than buy? You make more profit when you think up many good words, increase your production, and sell your products to many people. It is more important to give positive energy to to others than to receive it.

By words, I mean energy. If you can refuse evil words, the positive energy in yourself won't be lost. Again, if you accept words that create happiness, the positive energy within yourself will increase more and more. The wonderful words that you give to others have two or three times more power than the energy that you receive from others. This is the law of the universe; this is truth. Therefore, give all that is within you.

Don't criticize your children, your husband, or your wife. You must not take in any prejudices, nor must you give any name to these prejudices: an idiot, a fool, a good-for-nothing, a lazy person, a liar, a beast! The person you call a name will eventually become that name. Even if you may think these thoughts a little, never throw such words directly at people. You should be thoroughly aware of the awesome energy a word carries.

Say such words as these to those you love: 'I need you from my heart.' 'I depend on you.' 'You are essential to me.' 'You are wonderful.' 'You are bright and cheerful.' 'You are gentle and kind.' 'You are beautiful.' 'You are smart.' 'You are talented.' 'You are generous and forgiving.' 'You are caring.' ... Use such positive words abundantly to your children, your husband, or your wife. Then they will promptly become worthy of these words.

Always praise and admire your child. Always praise and admire your wife or husband. Always praise and admire your father and mother. Always praise and admire your friends and acquaintances, your neighbors and all people.

Always curb and restrain words of anger. Always curb and restrain words of jealousy. Always curb and restrain words of suffering. Always curb and restrain words of sorrow.

Why do we not think of others' hearts? Your words have thorns. Sharp words, even if uttered for the benefit of others, will make people react negatively. They will not allow your words to enter their hearts. How can you hurt another's heart and satisfy your own? How strange that is! Learn to feel your own pain more; cultivate empathy and nourish a heart that can understand another's pain.

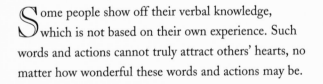

Some people show off their verbal knowledge, which is not based on their own experience. Such words and actions cannot truly attract others' hearts, no matter how wonderful these words and actions may be.

When you utter words which reinforce the truth – that every human being is divine and luminous – and when you also utter words that inspire others' souls, then you have made others truly alive.

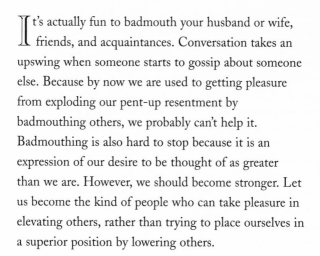

It's actually fun to badmouth your husband or wife, friends, and acquaintances. Conversation takes an upswing when someone starts to gossip about someone else. Because by now we are used to getting pleasure from exploding our pent-up resentment by badmouthing others, we probably can't help it. Badmouthing is also hard to stop because it is an expression of our desire to be thought of as greater than we are. However, we should become stronger. Let us become the kind of people who can take pleasure in elevating others, rather than trying to place ourselves in a superior position by lowering others.

If everyone in this world began in the same way to speak only words of love, what would the world be like? Speaking words of love means that all the energy works actively toward the positive. It means talking of happiness, prosperity, and health, and never talking about misfortune, illness, poverty, and so forth, no matter what. Word is alive. Word is energy. Word has the power to create. Everything is determined by word.

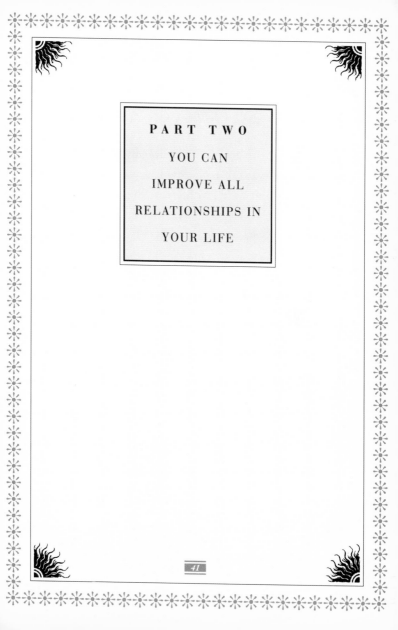

PART TWO

YOU CAN

IMPROVE ALL

RELATIONSHIPS IN

YOUR LIFE

BETWEEN MEN AND WOMEN

In marriage, two entirely different individuals encounter each other, unite, and create a new world. While interacting with, respecting, recognizing, forgiving, and helping each other, they gradually attain harmony and perfection together. It is as if the void that existed when each was alone and arid starts to heal as it is filled little by little. This process resembles the way the two totally different atoms, hydrogen and oxygen, encounter each other to create a new material called water.

Unless one blossoms more beautifully than before through marriage, it cannot be called true marriage.

Essentially, marriage should offer freedom, not restraint. One ought to be far freer in marriage than when alone. This is real marriage. Because people don't understand this, many marriages fail. The two people must share more freedom than before with each other, and continue to give more freedom to each other. Each partner must value his or her own freedom, and equally respect the other's freedom.

Husband and wife are like mirrors. If you reflect your spouse and find an ugly image there, you cannot blame him or her, because that ugliness is projected by your own thought.

Husband and wife are like the hands of a clock. Only when the long and short hands are perfectly balanced can the clock fulfill its purpose of telling the time. If either one of the hands tries to exert itself, ignoring the work as a whole and working on its own accord, the clock won't be able to tell the correct time. In the same way, husband and wife must harmoniously advance the clock of life together in the flow of the whole universe.

You never encounter the same person twice, for everyone perpetually changes second by second. This even applies to parent and child, husband and wife, brother and sister. You are wrong in grabbing the past image of a person and thinking that what you see now is the same person you saw in the past. Of course, it is also a fact that you too are changing second by second. You should live with this fact strongly imprinted on your mind: All human beings are constantly renewing themselves.

How many couples and lovers have the illusion that they love each other deeply? Their love, if probed, merely turns out to be self-love, because there is always fear and anxiety within themselves. This is not true love. People who have true love are totally devoted and can offer all of their lives to the ones they love. Among such people there is neither fear nor anxiety; there exists in them only the joy of mutual support and devotion. Love makes you selfless. For those who love, death no longer exists.

If you forever continue to be obsessed by your own failures as well as your husband's, wife's, or children's past behavior, weaknesses, and so forth, you will recall and repeat similar failures. Every one of those failures, events, and shortcomings belongs to a past that has already disappeared. Each tomorrow is absolutely new, and your radiant future is about to begin. However, if you constrict yourself with your own thoughts and feelings, refuse to forgive, criticize your husband's, wife's, or children's past, tremble with fear that the same may be repeated, and carry those past memories with you forever – then you will never attain true peace. No matter how large failures and shortcomings are, they are of the past and are gone and vanished. Take courage and change your thinking, trusting in your family's wonderful future, and firmly sever yourself from past events with your own will.

Man's history has been one of battles. Woman's history has been that of bearing and raising children.

Battles do not require any of the virtues needed for child raising – such as selfless and devoted love, compassion, benevolence, affection, gentleness, and patience. On the contrary, these virtues are in the way on a battlefield. If, during a battle, love and benevolence toward the enemy rise in the heart, there won't be a battle. War requires hatred, anger, fear, cruelty, conquest, and destruction.

Since the world's history has evolved as man's history of war, the human race is far from attaining peace. For this very reason, women have to truly awaken and then, for the first time, they can make the world peaceful. World peace depends on each woman's merciful heart.

c h a **5** *p t e r*

BETWEEN PARENTS
AND CHILDREN

Children are by nature remarkable. They have the ability to adapt immediately to any environment, they recover very well, and they absorb freely; they have keen sensitivity and are naturally capable of seeing into people's minds. They are also gentle, caring, and loving. All children are this way by nature. This is only natural, because children were born into this world bringing with them everything from heaven. If these remarkable children are damaged, it is done by the adults who surround them. No matter what child I see, I never overlook the child's best point and always praise him or her for it. I can never forget that child's truly happy face.

Each child is born with a wonderful innate talent. Whether this natural talent can develop depends on the parents. Compare parents who notice only their children's shortcomings and always nag them or raise their voices, with parents who find as many strengths as possible and keep praising their children. The children of the latter type achieve far greater development. All children have strengths and shortcomings. If you help their strengths grow instead of taking notice of their shortcomings, your children will develop perfectly.

Why can't you believe in your child? Why don't you try to trust your child? How pitiful for both parent and child! A foolish mother tries to maneuver her child as she desires. Instead of rebelling, the sad child makes an effort to follow the maneuvering. Both parent and child are wrong. They have lost sight of truth. More than anyone else, the mother should strongly believe in her child – as a child of God. Then the child without fail will try to respond to the trust. That trust should be the core in raising a child. If parents cannot believe in their own child, who will? Unless the parents have that trust, the child will never become independent. Independence is possible only when there is parental trust.

We think children are too young to know anything; this is a misconception. Children understand things well – not through learning, knowledge, and experience, but at intuitive, spiritual levels. Children can put greater inner wisdom and inspiration to work than adults can. Although children may appear as if they don't understand, they do, in fact, understand everything very well. It is important to listen well to what children say.

Parents should discern their children's true nature. You should raise your children so that the wonderfulness that is intrinsic to each of them is drawn out. Never compare your children with someone else's. Children are all different from one another. Your children have both strengths and shortcomings. See only their strengths, and help develop them. Parents must not have doubts about their children. Parents must not be confused and lose their way. Praise the wonderful qualities of each of your children and rejoice with them.

Emotionally scolding, blaming, and punishing your children is, in truth, only turning them away so that you will not be bothered and troubled by them. This is nothing but self-defense in disguise. The emotion that springs from you is, in fact, directed at yourself, never at your children. When disciplining your children, first put your emotions in order; then do it calmly.

The moment children feel that they are not loved deeply by their parents, they begin to demand constant parental attention. They learn that the more tricks and mischievous things they do, the more parental attention is concentrated on them – to an excessive degree. This is the beginning of delinquency. At this stage, parents must first show unconditional love before telling children not to do such things and trying to convince them that they shouldn't. If you understand deeply why your children have reached this point, the problem can be solved instantly. What absolutely no one in this world can live without, young or old, man or woman, is love.

Children sense very well their parents' worries, whether pains or agonies in the heart, sleepless nights, or a string of daily problems. It's better to convey your worries honestly to your children than to conceal or camouflage them. Trying to cover up the situation with false smiles does not convince children; it only increases their uncertainties. They intuitively grasp the situation with precision. Children are wonderful friends that parents can turn to for support.

Already before birth, human beings are different from one another. The circumstance of conception and the life inside the mother's womb differs from person to person. Some receive gentle parental love, hear affectionate words of gratitude, and arrive into this world amid prayers. To these new lives, parents convey hope and joy. Others, on the contrary, receive resentment from their parents and hear words of despair about their birth. Already before birth, they are showered with curses and hate that hamper their birth. I'm sure you can see just how much each baby's growth depends on the parents' own mental and spiritual being.

Even if your child is mentally retarded or physically weak, or has some other kind of mental or physical handicap, do not grieve and lament so much. And do not blame and torture yourself. It is not your fault, nor is it your child's. Since the purpose of the child's condition is to manifest the will of God through the vessel of the child, your child is not hurt as much as you are grieving over it. Your child was born carrying some kind of handicap because the inner soul of the child was willing to go through the process. Therefore, all you need do is pray for the divine missions of the child to be accomplished. That is all that's needed. Your child will, no doubt, face each difficulty with confidence and self-respect, and your child is the soul which can do that.

Some fruits ripen early; others ripen late. Only ripe fruit can fall to the ground. Children's independence can be likened to this. They should be kept in the care of parents until they are perfectly ripe. If parents hasten the children's independence and throw them out before they are ripe, they will never perfect themselves. An unripe fruit clings to the tree, and the tree also is attached to that unripe fruit.

Human beings are constantly attracted to character and talent superior to their own and, inspired by them, heighten themselves and polish their own talents. By observing the parents' behavior, children gradually reflect their parents' characters. The way parents live is the key to the development of their children's character. The family is a crystallization of society, the nucleus of the nation.

c h a  *p t e r*

BETWEEN YOU AND OTHERS

You were given a precious life in this world, with ties with your parents, brothers and sisters, teachers and students, friends and acquaintances. Whether these ties turn out to be good or bad, you will fulfill your life by polishing yourself through such relationships and improving yourself through your own efforts.

You will never again be born in the same environment. The same family construction will never again be repeated. As long as you are given, in this life, this environment and these human relationships, it's important to wholeheartedly value them. Precious relationships with family and friends are short and intense and last only in this lifetime, so you should make them deeply memorable and wonderful for as long as you live.

You need not express your opinions. You need not try to shine. You need not assert your existence. It suffices that you are there silently. Just be there, listen to others with sincerity, and be moved from your heart. That is enough. For people gather around the one who sincerely listens to them.

If you challenge a person who is hostile to you in order to get even with him or her, ultimately you are only destroying yourself. The rebound of vengeance always strikes and destroys you.

If you want to have good friends, rather than trying to get people interested in you, first take an interest in others.

When you release others, you release yourself from your own shackles.

———

Don't be a sycophant. Don't kowtow to others. It's disgusting to see. You should honestly and proudly express yourself through sincere words, actions, and attitudes, and be liked for who you truly are. You can't find a worthwhile person among those who act obsequiously to higher or more powerful people, while behaving insolently to lower or weaker people. Treat all people equally.

———

How others behave toward you should not affect your behavior toward them. You must not answer arrogance with arrogance. You must not answer sarcasm with sarcasm. You must not answer contempt with contempt. No matter how others behave toward you, always respond with warm love and a caring heart.

We must not treat the sick, the lonely, the weak in heart with pity. They have pride deep down in their hearts. Pity brings a reverse reaction. Because people refuse to open up to others and keep closed, they become ill, lonesome, and weak. Because they are proud, they obstinately shut themselves in their own shells and, unable to open up to others easily, they are at a loss. Like others, they too wish to liberate their hearts. For that to happen, it's important to avoid hurting their pride.

If one gives little, one receives little.
If one gives much, one receives much.

Others are others; you are you. Unless you keep telling yourself this over and over, it's clear that you will suffer from the doubt that germinates in your heart. It seems simple, but in fact it's very difficult to practice this. It becomes nearly impossible when you're put to the test. Unless you have great confidence and determination, before you realize it jealousy flames up. That's because you compare yourself with others. Go away, evil thought!

When you are hurt by others, insulted, or made a fool of, it's quite meaningless to resent or criticize them. You have unconsciously allowed others to hurt you for a long time and have given others the power to hold you down. This is directly the result of your unconscious behavior. You have unknowingly acted subserviently to others because you lack confidence and faith in yourself. It's crucial to wake to your own inner divinity and make yourself invincible.

Never defend yourself. Make no excuse. Defensiveness and excuses do not become you. Smoothly recognize your wrong, apologize, and give thanks to God. Then you will be evaluated as a great person. The more you run away, the smaller you become. How dare you transfer your responsibility to others! A great person is one who can take all the responsibility alone.

Most people feel personally attacked when criticized. As long as we live, we cannot avoid being criticized by others in some form. Whether you give criticism or advice, you should never violate this rule: No matter what the topic, you should never criticize in such a way that you stab the bull's eye – a person's most sensitive spot. You should help the person pay attention to the problem at a distance from the bull's eye. If you give another person criticism or advice that hits the target, the person won't listen to your criticism or follow your advice. Much worse, he or she will reject what you say, and your effort will end up having a reverse effect. This is an iron rule that applies even to your closest friend. It also applies to husband and wife, parent and child.

Don't harm yourself or others by unnecessarily exaggerating errors you or others made. Instead, exaggerate and praise the smallest good deed, whether it's yours or others'. Then people will overlook your errors and recognize your smallest good deed.

Behave proudly before no one, show anger to no one, scold no one, restrict no one, resent no one, badmouth no one, hate no one, sadden no one, criticize no one, hurt no one, discriminate against no one, betray no one, be jealous of no one, forgive everyone – this is how we should always hope to be.

As long as we are members of society, we cannot live without associating with others. In many cases, we cannot avoid associating with people we don't like. The damage we may experience in such relationships does not come from the fact that we have to associate with these people. The problem comes, rather, from our own attitude when we associate with them. If we treat them with the right attitude, in a way that corresponds with their personalities, abilities, and intellect, we will not receive any damage from them in any way. We go wrong when we try to present ourselves as more generous, good, and understanding than we are. Never make that mistake. You are not damaged by those with whom you associate; you are damaged only by your own wrong attitude.

How are we to surmount tragedy or despair that suddenly confronts us? By having friends to whom you can safely open up your heart and with whom you can share your pains, as they share theirs with you. To share your heart, you need to have deep mutual trust in your daily relationships. Make close friends in whom you can confide.

———◆———

How do you measure trust? By the level of sincerity. It's not measured by excellence in work, high intellect, or keen sensitivity. People who inspire our trust are people who have the character to treat others with unwavering sincerity.

———◆———

Y ou are not lonely because you are alone. Many are lonely amid their families and friends, or even with their beloved. Loneliness is a state in which one's heart is not fulfilled. Even when they live alone, those who somehow contribute to others harbor no loneliness in their hearts. If you don't want to be lonesome, be of service to others – whatever that service might be.

A human being, by nature, can become one with any other human being, no matter who. To achieve that, you must remove your ego from yourself – from your framework. Then you can understand another's heart; you can take it in your hand and read it like a book. When you understand another's heart, you can know your true Self for the first time.

What we fear most is the moment when we lose the feeling that our existence is valuable. When nobody pays attention to whether or not we exist, we taste unbearable humiliation and isolation. It's totally useless to blame others for this, for the cause is in yourself, even if you are not aware of it. Your attitude or vibration is gloomy or dark or rejecting of others. To become a human being who is loved, liked, and sought after by everyone, you need to behave as cheerfully as possible.

Let me give these words to those of you who have people in your life whom you don't like: If you always consider them your enemies, they will always be enemies to fight against; if you approach them with an open heart, as their comrade, they become allies.

Some people constantly grieve over their circumstances and their upbringing and talk only about their own problems to get others' sympathy. At first people show sympathy and pity, but that kindness usually doesn't last long. Eventually they will feel bothered and will try to avoid such complainers. Complaint itself bothers others. You should be well aware that, by nature, people are attracted to cheerful and positive topics, and dislike dark and melancholy topics.

Y ou must not be the kind of person who crushes others' spirits, who makes others' spirits dark. At times you think you don't at all mean to be that way, yet the atmosphere you project clouds people's spirits. Atmosphere is created by a person's daily thoughts. The person who always continues to have cheerful and constructive thoughts creates a warm, comfortable atmosphere that other people enjoy being near. You must become a person who radiates this kind of atmosphere.

People who emanate powerful hostility toward you, face you with evil intentions, and challenge you to combat fully believe you to be their enemy. However, when you probe deeply, you find that they are struggling with their own egos. On the surface, their combative thoughts seem directed toward you, but in fact they are directed toward themselves. Therefore, no matter what thought is directed at you, you need not fear. All thoughts return to the person who projects them. They never stay to harm you – as long as you don't catch them.

External help makes people weak. When you encourage yourself, bend before nothing, and give yourself strength, then your spirit is indeed noble. When you wish to give others a helping hand, you need to think it over carefully. If your help causes them to lose their independent spirit, your assistance has a negative effect. Be fully aware that we can open up our path of life only with our own hands.

You are truly mature if you can listen lightly, as if to an echo, to criticism or to vile blasphemy, no matter how unbearable, without reacting. As long as you are not attached to fame, glory, reputation, or social status, there is no need to suffer. A person without attachments has neither lifelong enemies to overthrow nor any need to flatter people in power.

Every single human relationship in this world exists as a process for spiritual advancement. People attract each other in order to reveal and manifest the unknown parts that exist within each of them; they learn from each other to draw out each other's inner self. This is true for all relationships – husband and wife, brother and sister, company director and employee, teacher and student, parent and child, friends and acquaintances.

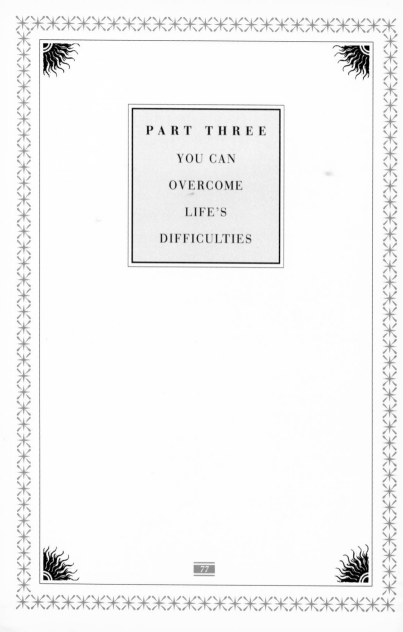

PART THREE

YOU CAN
OVERCOME
LIFE'S
DIFFICULTIES

c h a  *t e r*

HEALING YOURSELF
TO PERFECT HEALTH

For those of you who are suffering from illnesses, and for those of you who cannot be cured either by doctors or medicines, here is your remedy: Praise your body right now. Thank your body. If you have a liver problem, apologize to your liver for having overtaxed it selfishly without either care or thanks. Pledge to change your attitude and use your liver with sincere and deep gratitude. This applies to every bodily function, every internal or external organ, every artery or vein, every muscle or bone. If you continuously thank any part of your body, it will definitely respond. Miraculously, even stubborn diseases will be naturally cured.

Medicine, exercise, dieting, acupuncture, herbal remedy, and massage may be necessary to some extent to maintain your health. However, once anxiety or fear germinates, will your old way of health maintenance be sufficient? I would say no. Train your mind and spirit before training your body. If you are hurt, irritated, and driven by worry and anxiety over each trivial event, your health methods will be useless. You need first to nourish your mind and spirit so that, no matter what happens around you, you will be able to deal with it properly without hurting or wounding yourself. So long as your inner being is constant and shining with splendor, your body will be perfectly healthy – even if you do nothing about it. It's important to know that your physical condition originates from your inner being.

Why do we need to worry about illness – this illness and that, which we don't even have? This is nonsense. It's a waste of time and energy. It is you yourself who will be hurt by unnecessary worry. Either you have too much spare time in which to worry, or you are flooded with so much information that your judgment is impaired. It's understandable that you might worry about the illness you have; it's nonsense to fear the diseases that you don't have.

It's not too late. Promptly stop needless worrying. Instead of using all your energy for yourself, you need to turn your eyes more toward the love of mankind. Then you will no longer trouble yourself about foolish matters.

If you use your inner energy in a correct direction and in a correct way, you will never know fatigue. Not only that, your energy will be inexhaustible. The moment you hold back or try to spare the energy within you, it will stagnate and bring fatigue to your body, ultimately leading to illness.

By nature, the body has the power to revivify itself. You forget all about this principle and seek help in doctors and medicine. In doing so, you miss the chance to demonstrate this radiant, inherent power of resuscitation, and thus allow it to weaken. Next time, why don't you resolve to give a chance to that power within yourself?

The secret key to health: Don't think about illness in your mind; don't talk about illness with your mouth; don't listen to illness through your ears; and don't see illness with your eyes.

When people who are ill entertain various fears and anxieties, keep them pent up inside and are unable to get rid of them, their illness may worsen, or they may suffer and be in more pain than others would be. If you find sick people who are suffering badly or are seriously ill, know that their hearts are heavy, wounded, and anxious. If you listen to their worries and pains and try as much as possible to lift fear from their hearts, their pains and sufferings will miraculously disappear and they will gradually get better.

Illness does not come to you; you attract illness. Illness is also one kind of self-manifestation.

A doctor does not cure your illness. The doctor is merely a guide for climbing a mountain. The one who climbs is always you. You are the lead character. Unless you have the will to climb, you cannot climb to the top.

Natural healing power can be demonstrated equally by everyone. For those who have absolute faith in it, a greater power beyond imagination will be demonstrated. However, for those doubting people who cannot believe in it, that power works only weakly. Such people should go ahead and depend on doctors, without doubt or fear, because, in essence, medical science is there to help natural healing power.

Progress in medical science today is remarkable. Many effective drugs and injections are available on the market. However, recently there have been cases in which illnesses recur again and again precisely because of medicines and injections that work too well. For example, stomach and duodenal ulcers can now be easily cured by medicine without surgery. However, in many cases, people get ulcers again shortly after returning to work. Why? Because the cure of the inner state of being is completely neglected. Since the patient wants to alleviate the pain and suffering as much as possible, an easy method is taken. In the past, overcoming illness had the same exact meaning as strengthening and training the inner being. Those who could not fortify the inner being did not quickly recover from illness. Everyone, through having illness, learned unconsciously that illness had a purpose. By learning this, they first cured their inner state of being, and then the illness was cured. Today, however, since it is no longer necessary to cure our inner state of being to cure the illness, we lack spiritual growth and training. And that is why, even if an illness is cured once, it will recur again and again.

The most serious cause of illness that we may face as we proceed to the twenty-first century is increasing human isolation.

Human beings rarely die of fatigue or exhaustion. They die when mental fatigue and exhaustion lead to stress, then to illness. When the mind is constantly filled with tension, obligation, duty, and responsibility, humans have no time to breathe. Deadly serious people are apt to fall into this trap. It's important to finish quickly jobs that have to be done and to discard things immediately that do not matter much, and to keep what is in our mind in neat order. In this way, we can have extra space in our mind so that we can put out the greatest energy and concentration when needed.

It's absolutely natural for human beings to be healthy. There should be no need for special methods or efforts to be healthy. However, recently it seems as if that is not enough. Fewer and fewer people call themselves healthy. Why is this? It is because excessive information and knowledge flood this world. Information and knowledge have confused the natural needs of the body. We try to control our bodies with knowledge, rather than with the natural needs of the body. This throws our bodies into confusion, dulling our body's natural selection process, needs and responses.

Medicines are for the body. Prayers are for the soul. Medical science is for those ill in the body. Religion is for those who are ill in the soul. People think that curing the body and curing the soul are two separate things. However, physical illness cannot occur unless the soul is ill. Prayer is for cleansing the soul and for removing the illness from the inner state of being. If you find yourself physically ill, you can seek help from a doctor and medicines. But that's not sufficient. Pray. Pray to cleanse the illness in your mind, heart, and spirit, and the soil on your soul. Then, the illness in your body will be completely healed.

Everyone carries feelings that cannot be expressed to others: suppressed secrets and troubles, pain and shame, resentment and anger. Some can release all these feelings. They are open people who never close their hearts. Such cheerful people don't easily contract illness. The reason is that they don't hold their pains forever in their troubled hearts and moan over them. People become ill because they never try to talk about the trouble in the depths of their hearts. It's best to get whatever it is in your heart off your chest. This is particularly necessary for those recuperating from illness. How refreshed they will feel! It will lift the burdens from their hearts.

Never slight your body. Never defile it. Your body is divine and omnipotent. Reflect on your body. If you are ill, out of harmony, or not perfect at this moment, that's the result of unconsciously violating your body over a long period of time. If you change your way of thinking, recognize your body as a sacred and precious vessel, love it consciously, and care for it, then it will immediately demonstrate its perfection.

c   h   a   p   t   e   r

OVERCOMING STRESS, FEARS, AND PAINS

As long as we live, we confront difficulties and unbearable obstacles – at some point more than once. When you do, never say such cry-baby, silly things as 'I'm stuck', 'I'm completely cornered', 'I don't know what to do', or 'I can't see what's ahead.' Face the problems with words like 'There will be a way somewhere', 'I'll do my utmost', 'There's nothing I can't do', and so forth. If you confront any problem without running away, a path will easily open up. Don't block the road with fear before you face the problem. God will give you what you need when you need it.

No matter how oppressed, how physically weak you are, how poorly talented you may seem, you can certainly crawl out of that state. However, this happens only when you notice the state and question it: 'This kind of condition forever cannot possibly be right. Something is wrong somewhere. Is it others? Or is it me?'. At this point, if you blame others for your condition, how sad it is for you, because you will never redeem yourself in your life. Only when you hold yourself responsible can you crawl out of your present circumstances.

The more impatience we feel when trying, in fear and anxiety, to escape difficulties and adversities, the farther we stray from the true path. When we stop being impatient, stop trying frantically to escape, and calm ourselves, we hear the inner voice of guidance. That voice is always trying to reach us.

When all stress is gone, how peaceful and happy we must be! No matter where we are, we are always troubled with extreme tension, anxiety, and fear – which leaves us with no peace of mind. Even when we are asleep, forgetting everything, our tensions continue in our dreams, and sometimes we have nightmares.

If stress is totally eliminated from your mind, the illness and discord that you have had until now disappear in an instant. You can conquer stress with your own power. Recognize your own capacity as it is. Accept it without resistance. Don't overestimate or underestimate yourself – both can cause stress. Have absolute faith and confidence in the wonderful ability that is inherent in human beings. Wake it and demonstrate it in this world. In short, faith in yourself is the best medicine.

ailure does not exist in this world. No monster by the name of failure will attack you suddenly. It's only that an idea of failure exists within your mind. Failure itself has neither power nor meaning. Failure itself is not a failure – it's merely a precious experience. Advance to the next step by making use of this experience. What is success and what is failure is a matter of self-evaluation and is of no concern to others. Even if you have broken up your marriage, become bankrupt, flunked your exams, it's not appropriate to call the event itself a failure. Reflecting on the event, you have merely called up the idea of failure in your mind. If, however, you can make the event the motivation toward the next step, the event is never a failure. It was merely one point on the path to success that you had to pass by.

Innumerable people are standing in unfortunate positions due to their own ignorance and folly. They don't understand what attitude they should live with daily and how to deal with various difficulties. Those who neglect truth, or who don't try to know truth, can never be free from misery.

To those of you who are depressed, I would like to say: How did you fall into depression? Why are you still in that condition? You yourself know the answer. Right. Because you can think of nothing but yourself, and you direct all the energy you have toward yourself. Self-pity, self-criticism and anger toward yourself; the craving to draw sympathy, protection, and support from others; and the frustration over not easily getting such help – these are the causes. If you really wish to liberate yourself from depression, turn your self-directed energy toward others, even just a little. Dedicate that energy to others. Be of service to others. Don't give yourself idle time or a spare moment to think. Keep busy. Concentrate on how you can please others and put your ideas into practice. Start with those closest to you who surround you right at this moment. Until now, you've been asking yourself how you can please and satisfy yourself. If you really wish to get the answer, find ways to please others and practice doing so. If you continue this effort, you will certainly realize that you are filled with happiness. No matter how old you are, have a worthy purpose in life.

Ego is the source of every unhappiness, every suffering, every failure, and every pain.

There are some people in this world who accept their sad destinies. They take for granted that it is natural for them to suffer one misfortune after the other, as if convinced that they deserve it and must endure it with patience. Some of you might even praise these people for being able to do that. However, such people are, in fact, only inviting continuous misfortune and despair themselves in order to satisfy their own guilt. Unless you sever the guilt that lies latent in the depths of your mind and heart, you will attract misfortune forever.

When we receive an intense shock to our heart, our first impulse is to run away from where we are: We want to leave the place instantly, we wish never to return to the same place, and we wish never again to be around the person who hurt us. But this is not a constructive way of thinking. No matter what happens, we need to start by acknowledging that pain or shock. Face it directly and go through it without avoiding the pain. Otherwise, it's difficult to truly recover. What you run away from follows you all your life. Running away solves nothing.

Stop being infantile. Stand up firmly. Stop being gloomy and worried. Clean yourself up.

It's a big mistake to think that others will serve you whatever meal you need. If you depend on others to serve you, you will never have an opportunity to rise above your troubles. You must overcome your troubles with your own power. Your will to overcome them is what's important. Strongly believe that you can do it. It is you who loses when you keep babying yourself.

When you are obsessed with one anxiety, one problem, one trouble, or one affliction, and when you are preoccupied with that one thing for a long time, you are far from solving it; the anxiety, grief, or problem grows all the more within you. The best solution is to concentrate on diverting your mind from the problem, trying to envision the wonderful, cheerful, pleasant things to come after it is solved. Then, before you know it, the problem will be naturally solved.

You are not the only person who shoulders suffering as you live. You are not the only one who from time to time finds work burdensome. You are not the only one who thinks it would be wonderful if you could give up everything and live in freedom. In this world, everyone, young or old, man or woman, lives more or less with similar suffering. Those who shine are those who try to live for the human race while carrying their own burdens. Yes. If you forget your personal pain and work positively with courage for the human race, your pain will easily disappear.

By firmly convincing yourself that your present suffering is not totally meaningless, that you go through it for some definite, necessary reason, you can overcome that pain.

When confronting a problem, people always say, 'Well, I've tried to do what I can...'. To me, having tried only what one can is giving up midway, and is no different from not trying at all. With this kind of thinking, there will be no sign of any improvement. Unless you carry your effort right through to the very end, no path will open. If you have the will to carry it all the way through, even the most tightly closed door, even the heaviest iron door will yield a narrow space that will allow a ray of light to go through. If the door opens even the tiniest crack, the rest is in the bag. Just wait patiently for the right time to come. The path you have envisioned and constantly wished for will definitely open up.

As everyone says, life is like mountain climbing. When climbing with a high peak as a goal, some go smoothly, others lose their way or wander into the woods, and still others fall into the valley. This corresponds in life to frustrations, failures, difficulties, or illnesses. However, this does not mean that everything is over. On the contrary, a wonderful opportunity is open for you to rediscover a new, shining, and level path that you were not able to see from the path you had been tracing earlier. A new path is always prepared in front of your eyes. All you need to do is switch to that new path.

ATTAINING WISDOM IN
LIFE, AGE, AND DEATH

Believe from the bottom of your heart in the astonishing wonder and miracle of the life force – nature's force. People are apt to believe in the wonder of medicine before believing in the wonder of the life force.

Don't fear life. Don't be anxious about living. Even if the body is not free, the inner being is free. Have hope. To live means constantly to hold a bright star of hope for the future. No matter what your endeavor, don't give up.

Thoughts of fear, affliction, and sorrow produce deterioration, while thoughts of joy, love and hope produce life.

In the process of birth and growing up, the key to life is how much we absorb and digest. In the process of aging, the key to life is how many superfluous things we discard and how simple we become.

Age is a ripening of experience. It is such a dignified path that even the most outstanding youth cannot come close to following it.

I don't want to call those of you advanced in years 'old people'. I would like to call you guides, teachers, masters, pioneers, or long-distance runners completing the race. I praise you for having lived safely till now.

You should be praised for having lived without stopping your lives in the middle of the course. I understand how rugged and agonizing the path has been that led you to this point. Having lived up till now – that itself is already enough to make you worthy. There is no need to say more. There is no need to tell more. Everyone around you understands. The deeply carved year-rings of life show the way you have lived. No matter how you have lived your life, it is the strength in your own inner being – and not others – that has enabled you to live safely up to now. Those whose inner state of being is weak would have lost their lives before reaching this point. You are strong people. You are successful people. You are reliable people. You are wonderful people. I deeply respect you. From now on, please feel free to admonish and encourage young people. Please live on with pride in your heart.

When you must suddenly part with this world, questions may arise in your mind. Have you any regrets about the way you have lived? Have you been of enough service to your marital partner and your children? Have you done your best in your work? Have you sprinkled love, care, and kindness over people who surround you? Have you given daily thanks to God? If none of these things troubles your heart at all, you will leave no regrets behind you. However, if even one thing bothers you, know that it's not yet too late. Resolve to change your behavior in daily life so that, no matter when you die, no matter when you are called from this earth, it will be fine with you.

You needn't fear death. Death is what you live with from the moment of your birth. It's not that death comes to get you abruptly one day. Death is with you in life at all times. A drop of rain is created from a piece of cloud and falls on the mountaintop. Together with other drops, it forms a river and flows downstream. Where is the water going? To meet the sea. The sea is the final destination, the death, of the river. The moment the river meets the sea, it becomes one with the infinite. The infinite is not nothingness. It is the source which creates everything.

The river and the sea are never separate things. They are not to be thought of separately. Life and death, like the river and the sea, are connected. The sea water evaporates, becomes a piece of cloud, then again produces another raindrop. To return to death means to be reborn all over again.

Know well what life truly is. All of life is in the hands of God. It's true that whether one lives or dies depends on God's will. Whether one lives for a moment or for a hundred years is irrelevant, for life continues to live forever. Death merely means taking off the garment called the body. Ultimately, humans will die when they are to die, no matter what worldly measures they may take to avoid death. Those who are to live will live no matter how close to death they may be brought. We must not attach ourselves to life.

Neither fear death, nor fear living all alone. It's important to nurture the calmness of your own inner being that fears nothing at any moment.

Animals experience pain, but they do not have fear of death at all. Perhaps this is a unique emotion given only to humans. However, the degree of pain differs between those who meet death with fear and those who gladly accept death. You should know well that death is not a terror. Death is merely a process of leaving the body – shedding an uncomfortable, restricting garment and transcending spiritually to a shining, free world.

PART FOUR
YOU CAN LIVE YOUR
LIFE IN LOVE,
HAPPINESS,
FORGIVENESS, AND
HARMONY

LOVE OTHERS FIRST IF YOU WANT TO BE LOVED

The mother tries to protect and help her child in every way, even at the cost of her life. Perfect maternal love knows no fear. The mother tries to efface her ego and give up everything for her child. No, rather than try, she does it spontaneously and naturally. If you want to overcome all fears, you must carry out true love all the way – like the mother's. Love knows no fear; perfect love eliminates fear.

It is sufficient just to give love. All you need to do is continue giving love earnestly, seeking nothing and expecting nothing. You never have the right to force another to accept your love.

As long as we were born into this world, for whatever reason, we must continue to live. To live, we must be happy. To be happy, we must be loved. To be loved, we first must love others. By positively performing acts of love, for the first time we can be loved. Love can be a word or an action; it can even be silent, as long as there is unchanging compassion flowing in the bottom of the heart.

Every human being seeks love. Every human being wishes to be understood. Nothing is so painful as not being loved and understood by others. If this continues forever, we can even lose the hope for living. That's how much being loved and understood by others means to us – it gives us true joy and brings purpose to life.

Let me say to those of you who are neither loved nor understood by anyone and are downcast with loneliness and isolation: Think well why you are in this state. Yes, you've only been wishing yourself to be loved and understood by others; you have never thought of others at all. Loving and understanding others must come first.

Love is not trying to change another to suit you; love changes you to suit another. Love means accepting others just as they are and respecting and valuing them just as they are.

To lead a satisfactory life as a human being is to continue giving others as much love as possible.

Those who try to appeal to others and seek their help by playing a tragic role have not yet been paralyzed by their pain; they are still capable of dealing with it on their own. Although it might sound heartless, it is okay to listen to them with one ear or just leave them alone. On the other hand, those who are truly beaten down by agony distance themselves from people who will support them. Thinking they are not worthy of receiving help, they withdraw themselves from even close friends and family members. To those people – and their agonies – you must sincerely and wholeheartedly listen, even at the cost of your own precious hours.

Don't develop blind attachment, especially toward your marital partner or children, your parents, or your friends and acquaintances. Such attachment ultimately destroys others and strangles you.

Keep wishing to be loved by others. Keep wishing to be respected by others. Keep wishing to be sought after by others. Miraculously, while so wishing, you naturally start to acquire and develop a suitable character, because you begin truly to understand what to do in order to be loved and respected.

 p t e r

CREATE YOUR OWN HAPPINESS

Take a look at a person glowing with happiness.
What's different about that person? What a
gentle smile, what beautiful conduct, what a noble
heart, and what a cheerful and joyful atmosphere this
person radiates!

Probably such people do not judge others' conduct.
Probably they find good intentions in others. Probably
they have no contempt of others. Probably they find
only virtue in others and talk only about virtue. That
must be why they are always shining beautifully.

What hampers your happiness is not your husband, nor your wife, nor your children, nor your parents-in-law. What hampers you is yourself. No one else. Your wrong thoughts, emotions, and knowledge stand in your way. Happiness is not something that others give you. You must create it with your own hands. To do so, your mind and heart must always be one with God.

If you think that to become happy, you must make greater efforts than others, or that you are not worthy of happiness because of your past mistakes, you will never be happy - just as you thought.

Our hearts ache when we hear a sad story; we laugh out loud when we hear a joyous one. We shrink when we hear a scary story; we feel happy when we hear a happy one. Like yawns and the flu, bad and unpleasant things are infectious. At the same time, don't forget that happiness and health are also contagious. If you avoid dark or sad news in your daily topics and try to thrive on bright, cheerful topics, your family will always be filled with happiness.

I think you know very well that we cannot measure the degree of another's happiness or unhappiness by appearance. When people are content, they experience happiness and peace, and never find life unbearable no matter how poor their living conditions or health may be. Contentment comes from demonstrating your given power to the fullest by putting your whole heart and soul into everything you do. This contentment is proof of happiness.

Here at this very spot you must discard all your hate, give up your obsessions, wipe away your jealousy. Otherwise your unhappiness will only increase. Your violent emotion will hurt your mind and body even more painfully and drive you further into the depths. Every bit of unhappiness derives from your own thoughts and emotions. Discard all your hate right now. No matter how justified your reason for your hatred, still release it from your heart. If the smallest amount of hate remains in a corner of your heart, true happiness will never come.

Never think of yourself as an unfortunate human being. Also, never think you were born under an unfortunate star. If you drag such a thought behind you, you will never be able to sever yourself from unhappiness for the rest of your life. That is like gladly accepting unhappiness or being resigned to it. Even if unhappy situations occur one after another, still never think yourself unfortunate. As long as you think yourself an unfortunate human being, you are in a state of mind that does not allow you to exit from unhappiness. If you accept yourself as an unfortunate human being, that's the same as inviting unhappiness. Always say to yourself that you are never an unfortunate person, that you don't even want to think you're unfortunate, and that you can't possibly be unfortunate. No matter what happens, change your thoughts to light-filled, positive ones. Then unhappiness will run away by itself. Brighten all the corners of your heart so that no space is left for unhappiness to enter. Then the seed of unhappiness quickly withers before it germinates in the heart. It is your way of thinking that creates the source of unhappiness, invites unhappiness, and nurtures unhappiness all out of proportion.

Many people live in a nearsighted way, caught up by the gains and losses right in front of them. They never know how much happiness can come if they live with a broader perspective, rather than being swayed by what is before their noses. Better to be called a large vessel than a master of small crafts.

Conduct based on the wrong way of thinking produces only wrong results. When your way of thinking and your conduct align themselves with truth, this results in prosperity, happiness, and richness.

Happiness is everywhere. It is nearby, easily within reach. Happiness surrounds us at all times, already provided. It is never far from us, nor does it run away from us. In short, happiness exists within each of us.

Many, however, cannot attain happiness despite their search for it. Although happiness exists so close to seekers, people who do not understand what happiness really is cannot attain it easily. Happiness is not a certain unique and special condition. Happiness is something that always exists and shines with remarkable splendor among the ordinary experiences of life. Those who cannot attain happiness, in spite of their search, are the people who do not realize the happy spirit within their heart. People with a happy spirit can give sincere gratitude for every little thing in their daily lives. Their gratitude springs forth in their heart. Happiness will never visit those who do not have a spirit of gratitude in daily life.

The more good things you do for
others, the happier you become.
Divine light increases and fills your being.
A sense of fulfillment, satisfaction, progress,
and achievement rises in your heart which,
in turn, compels you to serve others all the
more. How great it will be when this can be
your natural way of life!

FORGIVE YOURSELF AND OTHERS TO FREE YOURSELF

To forgive others does not mean to obliterate everything from our memory. It is the principle of human emotion that the harder we try to forget, the more we will recall the unforgivable words or actions done to us. Then, why do we have to forgive others? To awaken peace in our own inner state of being.

If our hearts are always filled with hate, resentment, or jealousy, we are the ones who must suffer constantly – and not others. To lead our own hearts to freedom and peace, we must, of our own volition, free our hearts of hatred. This is forgiveness.

The act of forgiveness may appear to be
done for the sake of others, but it is an act
totally for the sake of ourselves. Forgiveness
means to banish from our own hearts every
bit of antipathy, every bit of anger, and
every bit of hostility.

———◆———

Why do we have such a problem with forgiving
others? Why do we have to spend our days in
darkness and agony? Where is the cause? It's in our
own hearts. We cannot forgive others because we
cannot forgive ourselves. We can't stand seeing our
pride being hurt – that's why we cannot forgive others.
The cause is not in others; it's in our own hearts.

———◆———

Small-minded people become angry from even a little criticism. Over-serious people blame others for minor errors and, even though they try to forgive them, can't do so easily. Even worse, if the problem has arisen from their own errors, they blame themselves all their lives and never see the light. Both behaviors are typical of small-hearted people. However, great people have hearts large enough to accept and forgive everyone and everything, even those who have criticized or betrayed them. We should try to be such people with large hearts.

You know yourself better than anyone else does. You also know why you fell into bad ways. Even if you might deceive people around you, you can't easily deceive yourself. You needed to attain something even at the cost of your high, clear, untainted humanity; and, after you obtained it, how miserably your self-blame fell upon you! It is a great pity to punish yourself for what you've done. You don't need to suffer so much; you have already suffered enough. Everything has vanished. The past is over. If you live correctly from now on, that's enough. Live cheerfully toward the future.

'I was bad', 'I was to blame', 'I was no good', 'I was imperfect', 'I was stupid' – if you constantly criticize yourself this way, all you get is illness. You not only make no progress, you fail to escape from the negative-thought vibrations. When you blame yourself, you are merely trying to experience a kind of self-satisfaction subconsciously. No matter what happens, you must live facing forward; otherwise, life is not worth living. No matter what happened in the past, everything can turn around through your heartfelt self-examination.

Let's make today the day we will discard all the burdens that we have dragged from the past. Let's courageously resolve to forgive everything. You may feel too much vexation to forgive so easily at this late point. You may feel that you cannot forgive until you have acted upon the hatred that you have shouldered for decades. You may feel you cannot forgive until the other party apologizes. However, it does no good to keep chaining yourself with these shackles. Boldly free yourself from them now. Forgive everything for your own sake. How much lighter your heart will be! It's you yourself who will gain the most, make no mistake about that.

You who are suffering from illness, from poverty, and from various misfortunes: Your thinking is wrong. Don't blame others. Don't blame yourself. Don't resent others. Don't resent yourself. People are not to blame. Neither are you to blame. Everything that happens is just the effect of a past cause working itself out and fading away. Know that truth well. Don't deviate from it.

There are some who worry too much about their shortcomings and refuse to forgive them. They are convinced that no suffering in the world is more serious than being troubled by their own shortcomings. What a pitiful life they must lead! To forgive yourself first and to love yourself is, indeed, truth.

Now, at this moment, you are released from all restrictions and restraints. You have become perfectly free. God knows everything about you; your sufferings, your pains, sorrows, and wrong conducts are in the past. God forgives everything, forgives everything about you. Yes. You are now free. Release yourself from your own shackles. Rejoice with all your heart and soul.

13

FOLLOW NATURE'S COURSE TO WHOLENESS AND HARMONY

I t's good to carry out everything by following the natural flow. Nature always brings things to us in the course of time, regardless of whether or not we are aware of it. Nature neither hastens nor becomes impatient. If we leave everything up to nature's course and harmonize with it, we can ride on the flow of time, and everything can work out smoothly.

If left alone, an open wound naturally forms a scab, and gradually the skin heals. Toxins (such as fatigue and poisonous elements) and unnecessary things are put out of the body through natural elimination and perspiration, restoring the body to its original state. If we live like this, obeying the natural course and not going against it, we will be able to live in accordance with the law of the universe. This law means returning to the original perfect Self – or, looked at more deeply, it means returning to your own divinity.

Everything from the beginning is destined to work out. All you need is to refrain from panic, impatience, insecurity, and fear. Calm yourself and know how to wait until the right time comes naturally.

Don't force. Relax more. The more force you apply, the greater friction you create, and this keeps everything from going smoothly. The more you're suffering, the more you should let go. Don't stop breathing. The greater the pain, the less you should clench your teeth. The more serious you become, the more you should relax your tension. Leave everything to nature. Because you try to do everything yourself, you end up forcing. Why don't you try to find the divine power that is present within you? Why don't you try to draw it out? It's not you but the divine power inherent within you that does everything.

God always speaks of truth to us through nature – in the sound of flowing water, in a gentle breeze blowing through the woods, in the singing voice of a bird, and in the beautifully blooming flowers.

Nothing can bring us back to nature more than being in nature and making contact with it. Let us gently close our eyes and listen to the voice of nature and communicate with it. No matter how busy we are, we must never forget to contact nature. Great nature is alive. Great nature exists by God's will, and it is formed by the law of the universe. When we meet with misfortune or disaster, the first thing to do is contact great nature. Nature will give us a breath of great harmony, pour energy into us, and make us notice that we still have room to grow and how insignificant our concerns are.

Nature is working upon us. Sun and water pour unlimited energy into us freely. Then what, indeed, are we giving back and returning to nature, sun, and water? Although it is crucial for us to melt into one with nature and harmonize with it, we are doing quite the opposite. We are destroying nature and arrogantly trying to master nature. Yet, still, nature silently tolerates the harm we are causing with our wilfulness. But can we truly get away with it? Once nature explodes, we will be totally helpless, no matter how abundantly we use our intelligence together. Nothing is more fearful than natural disasters. What causes cataclysms is nothing but our wrong thoughts and actions.

When the pond freezes up, it becomes unvaried and uninteresting. How wonderful it is that the water moves or flows! By flowing, water creates new shape after new shape with endless variety. Running water never stops for a moment. It moves on eternally. How full of life it is! It's alive. The water itself is alive and shining.

The human mind ought to be as fluid as flowing water. The mind that has become as stiff as ice is neither interesting nor joyful. It cannot produce anything new.

It's not good just to be delicate and sensitive, nor is it good just to be rough and coarse. You can't be considered a fine human being unless you achieve balance and moderation in every respect. The delicate and sensitive worry so much about others that they exhaust themselves. The rough and coarse ignore and irritate others' hearts too much. In everything, leaning too much to one side always makes you lose the balance. No good results come of it.

Intellect, emotion, and the senses are all important, but you should not lean toward any one of them. How wonderful it is when these three faculties are in contact and in harmony with one another!

A bird can fly freely in the sky because its wings on both sides work in good harmony. If it leaned only toward its right wing or applied too much force in only its left wing, it would not be able to soar. A truly great person likewise is one who can balance well. Even if the right side is correct, you should not be attached only to that side. Nor should you be too attached to the left side, even if it is the wrong side.

When a bird turns to the right, it puts its weight on its right wing. If the bird only kept its weight dead center at all times, it could only fly straight. Real balance, in the broadest perspective, is leaning sometimes to the right and sometimes to the left, thereby ultimately achieving harmony.

Especially in recent years, it has become quite difficult to find people who live in wholeness and naturalness. Everyone is forced to live in a fragmented way. How wonderful it would be if human beings could grow naturally, live naturally, love naturally, and blend into one with nature! People who live in naturalness are people who can live in wholeness. We must always see the whole, perceive the whole, and grasp the whole while we live. If you look at your partial self, you can see only a small, fragmented image of yourself. It's not good to deny your body just because you love spiritual life so much; it's also not good to deny the spirit or soul because you love materialism so much. Harmonizing and utilizing both the spiritual and the material to the fullest leads to a life of wholeness. And those who can live in wholeness are the happiest people in the world.

PART FIVE

YOU CAN UNCOVER
YOUR TRUE SELF
AND ACCOMPLISH
YOUR DIVINE
MISSIONS

14

WORK AND OPPORTUNITY

The future is always reaching out a new hand toward us. To grasp it firmly, we must always make a net of curiosity all around our daily lives so that we won't let opportunity slip through. All human beings are equally surrounded by wonderful fortune. Whether or not we turn our eyes toward this fortune depends on our attitude.

Opportunity is always in front of your eyes. There is hardly a person who has never had a single opportunity in life. It's just a matter of whether the person grasped it or not. Then how should one grasp opportunity? By living in accordance with the law of nature. Those who cannot attain opportunity are living against the law in some way. The law of great nature means to harmonize with everything on earth.

Taking pride in the job given to you at present is an important key to bringing great blessings in your future. Those who constantly complain and are discontented with their jobs are not welcome in their workplaces. They should quit instantly. I pity the workplaces that hold such people. Any place can change in any way according to your thinking. Even if where you find yourself now is not suitable to you, continue to make efforts to live with pride in your workplace. At a certain point, quite miraculously, you will find yourself truly proud of your work. Those who work with heartfelt pride in the job are always rewarded.

What should you do if you are suddenly confronted with illness, an accident, or a disaster, at the very moment when you must accomplish something, when everything is near completion, or when you have staked your life on the job? This is, in fact, the very moment when you can demonstrate fully your inherent power. You can, without fail, control your body mentally. You can definitely accomplish the task with your mental power. The more strongly you feel the responsibility to carry through your task, the greater power you can demonstrate; and you can actually accomplish it. However, if someone else is there to shoulder even a little of the work, or if you wish to depend on others to find some kind of solution through others' assistance, the inner power cannot be demonstrated, and you cannot avoid giving up your work in the middle.

At present you may be driven by an impulse to give up the work you have started. You may hate going to school. Or you may be feeling totally lazy about doing anything. This is the very moment when you need to overcome your frame of mind and push yourself forward just one more time. You need to strengthen your inner being so it will conquer every temptation. People begin to walk down the path of no return because they yield to a weak state of mind and immediately succumb to temptations. Continue to encourage your inner self.

People have said for years that overwork leads to illness. That is never the case, however. The more we work, the healthier we become – that's how we were meant to be. If you become ill from overwork, that is because illness was triggered by emotional instability, resulting from shocks to your system such as fear, worry, irritation, or mutual resentment and hate. Overwork never leads to illness. On the contrary, the more you work, the more limitlessly your inner energy flows out.

The primary cause of fatigue in work can often be found in your mental and emotional attitudes, such as boredom or resentment, restlessness and lethargy, and feeling that your abilities are not evaluated or appreciated properly. All these feelings are created by your own emotion within your body. As far as the brain is concerned, it can work after eight or even twelve hours as actively as at the beginning.

Always give yourself words that will inspire and encourage you. Those words will be your incentive to give you motivation for your next job or task. At the same time, your trite worries and troubles will blow away.

There is always someone somewhere in this world who is noticing you. Even if others do not acknowledge you now, you do not need to be impatient and frustrated. Whether others are looking at you or not, unwaveringly carry out whatever you should do. In time your chance to shine will definitely come.

Even if others think that you are not talented or competent, don't pity yourself so much. Others are others. You are you. There may be something that you can do and others cannot. In short, do not acknowledge your weak points. Instead, do acknowledge your strong points and develop them. There is always someone who is taking notice of your abilities.

Human beings work not for profit but for the joy of living through working.

KNOWLEDGE, INTELLECT, AND INTUITION

Knowledge is needed in our lives. However, if knowledge always runs ahead and the spirit lags behind, then that knowledge no longer serves its purpose. Knowledge can be useful in life and can assist people when they confront difficulties; but it can also complicate life and create new difficulties, hardships, and disasters. Unless we constantly try to harmonize knowledge and spirit, we cannot attain true happiness.

Knowledge is only knowledge. No matter how much more knowledge you accumulate than others, it is meaningless unless you absorb and express it in your own personality and behavior. Otherwise you are like an obese child. When an obese child eats and eats without being able to digest the food totally, the food eaten is merely wasted. If the child cannot change the food into energy that results in shining health and beautiful proportion, the food is not perfectly utilized. Lumps of flesh and lumps of fat form here and there, making the child's body out of proportion. It's the same with knowledge. Unless you digest it efficiently, you will turn into an overblown person who is vain about your knowledge.

All civilization and culture, including art, medicine, and other sciences, originate from divine wisdom. By no means do you need to reject everything you think is the opposite of nature. On the other hand, neither do you need to immerse yourself in these things. Wise people can walk the middle path, sometimes depending on medicine and civilization, and at other times not needing them. It is important to break through difficulties by using God-given wisdom that gives you the intuition and judgment appropriate to the time and place. Human beings should not live in a fixed, inflexible way that leans toward one extreme. We should always be flexible. This is possible only when one becomes an accepting person who can be grateful for everything.

No matter how much time you have spent acquiring knowledge, that knowledge is not your own true experience. You have merely accumulated other people's experiences and facts. They did not rise from within you. What you came to know through others is merely stored in your brain as knowledge. When the time comes to make critical decisions, such knowledge only stands in the way of intuition rising from within yourself. Those who have accumulated only knowledge are useless at such a moment.

Whether you are slightly superior or inferior to others in intellect, intelligence, talent, ability, and so forth is of no consequence. It's like comparing the size of acorns. It's not at all significant. However, virtue is another matter. The height, or depth, of virtue determines the quality of one's character. One should endeavor to become a person of virtue rather than a person of intellect. In the climb toward virtue, intellect is on a level several steps below.

The duller people are, the more half-baked smatterings of knowledge they pick up and show off. Because they are dull, they lack judgment and absorb everything passively. This leads to storing up all that half-baked knowledge in the depths of the subconscious.

When people become ill, despair, or fail, one after another of these smatterings rises to the surface of consciousness and constricts them tightly with trivial knowledge. They hypnotize themselves with their own dark thought, driving themselves into helplessness. This is nothing but folly.

It's wrong to assume that all knowledge is good to absorb. Take into yourself the kind of knowledge that makes you feel encouraged, filled with hope, and inspired with happiness for living. Consciously discard knowledge that leads you to darkness, anxiety, and fear.

One should become a person of virtue rather than a person of intellect. Knowledge and intellect sound good, and, surprisingly, many people get excited about knowledge and intellect. But, after all, knowledge is no more than the accumulation, or memory, of past experiences. Can one who has accumulated more knowledge than anyone else be called a wise and accomplished person? No. A superior person who is respected by many is a person of virtue, which is far beyond intellect.

When we're trying to create something new or trying to discover a clue to the solution of a problem, we focus our consciousness, ponder hard, and concentrate our efforts. But no matter how hard we try, we can hear only the noise of past knowledge and other accumulations within us. The sound of something new, something creative, or a clue to a problem all come from God.

Life is said to be a series of choices and decisions. We sometimes base our decisions on our experiences, knowledge, and information; but in the majority of cases we end up deciding by intuition. Simple feelings of likes and dislikes take precedence over experience or knowledge. We can live the lives we want much better if we follow our feelings. This is because intuition is an answer that flows to us from God.

After you have made your best efforts, release yourself completely from that problem. When you are taking a bath, or when you're appreciating trees and flowers in the garden, or when you're just relaxing, forgetting about everything, the answer will flash as an intuition. Not all problems are solved only by your daily efforts. Everything will be achieved only when human effort and divine wisdom become one.

Open your eyes. The visible world is not the only world. To truly know this, you must develop intuition and wake spiritually. If you do so, you will clearly see that the invisible world majestically exists, and that its connection with us can never be severed. With this awareness, you will be able to free yourself smoothly from the endless difficulties that have troubled you up till now.

LIVE FREELY FOR YOURSELF, KNOW YOURSELF, BE TRUE TO YOURSELF

What you need to do right now is to discover with your own insight a path of perfect freedom: freedom from mental constriction, freedom from physical fetters, freedom from the shackles of human relationships. You must be free in everything. You don't need to be bound by anyone. Live freely as you wish. Nothing is as worth living as the path you have chosen and determined by yourself.

We must never think that our past way of living is our only way to live. Many different ways of living exist in this world. If you are obsessed by conventional thought and can live only within its framework, you cannot obtain a truly secure way of life. Know the spacious, profound, and endless world. Fly bravely out of the world of convention. There you will find the unshakeable existence of the world beyond convention, where spiritually awakened people live in freedom and true peace.

Some people are too insecure to live without constant instructions from others. Lacking independence, they dance to what others say, not questioning such ways of living at all. Such people demean life and the divine missions of human beings. The first step toward awakenment is to know the truth: One determines one's own destiny. No one else can control it.

Narrow-minded, small-hearted, or self-centered people of limited outlook always react offensively and defensively when blamed, reprimanded, or warned by others – whether or not those criticisms are correct. They are desperate to protect and defend themselves. Large-hearted, unselfish people with a broad outlook are never shaken up no matter what happens; they don't even budge. They remain calm and don't even try to defend themselves. They let other people think as they wish, and they remain content. No matter how others view them, it's fine with them, because they know themselves very well.

Quite a number of people hide what they are, always trying to make themselves seem better than they are. They worry intensely about what others think of them, keep up appearances and formalities, and lead pretentious lives. They end up suffocating themselves. They neither know the joy of a life based on truth, nor have the incentive to create such a life. They dwell in a hollow world. They ought quickly to take off their stiff armor, return to their true naked selves, and live with vigor and freedom.

Take a new look at yourself. Return to your undisguised self. You should live without a mask. Return to your true self. What's so scary about showing your honest self? What do you fear? Why are you so afraid? How painful it must be to live constantly deceiving even yourself! With courage, return to your essential self. Illness and pain will disappear at that instant.

You cannot become anything but yourself. No matter how many pretensions you may have, you are you. Even if you suppress the real you and try to become someone totally different – because other people seem more wonderful in your eyes – you will not attract others. The most essential path is to act naturally just as you are, acknowledging your shortcomings for what they are. Knowing your true self, without any disguise or pretensions, and being able to express yourself is the path to happiness.

SHED THE PAST, LIVE NOW, HOPE FOR THE FUTURE

Become reborn completely new from this day on. The you who has worried unnecessarily about each and every thing no longer exists. Be the self who dreams about a bright tomorrow full of hope.

Let's put an end to small-mindedness. You have been concerned more than necessary about insignificant things. You have frayed your nerves by gloomily worrying over small matters all the time. You should be tired of such a self. Get rid of this past self.

If you make a great effort to change people around you, your effort will be wasted. If you want to change others, you must first begin to change yourself. Unless you make conscious efforts, it's not easy to change yourself. Because of many years of habit, you will swing back to your old ways before you know it. Complaint, discontent, and irritation are your thought habits. If you consciously try to exchange such negative thoughts with light-filled, positive thinking when they arise within you, you will notice that you are completely changed from your old self.

Human beings possess countless wrong ideas and concepts. Blind beliefs about themselves are particularly bad. Break the frame of self-limitation as soon as possible. Otherwise, for the rest of your life, you will not be able to accomplish what you should be able to accomplish.

Your character and your thoughts were formed on the basis of your past. They are the results of your past, as well as your reactions to the things accumulated in the past. Should you wish to change your character and thoughts, sever yourself from your past right now, and live this day completely anew.

Today is the result of yesterday and the cause of tomorrow.

Now is the time to bring out your hidden potential. It's now or never. Why are you so hesitant? Why are you so hung up on it? What is keeping you from instant action? There's no need to hesitate. Come, right now, on this very spot, start putting your thoughts and wishes into action. In the process, everything will start to fall into place. As long as you are only thinking, you can't actually accomplish anything.

You are being recreated every moment. You have no time to be troubled by past events. You must be too busy to regret anything, even for a second. Everything vanishes in this instant of rebirth. Wake to the realization that you are being reborn instantly – and acknowledge it.

Every moment is a new moment.

Truth exists in everyone and everything. How fast you realize and express it depends upon you. You are free to delay it, postpone it, or waive it forever. However, the moment you stop delaying it, even by one day, truth is there right now before your eyes. It has only been waiting for you to notice it.

Make use of this moment. Live this moment with all your might. Don't be stingy about using your energy. Bring forth all of it, and use all of it. Don't save any for tomorrow. Don't worry about tomorrow. If you live this moment perfectly, if you grasp something at this moment, then you have built the foundation of your future happiness for the rest of your life.

How did you become what you are today? How should you change yourself from what you are now? Your daily thoughts have been creating yourself as you exist this very moment. By changing your past mental habits to completely new ones, you can disconnect from your old self and start becoming a new self. New mental habits form by always thinking of God and by living cheerfully and positively with hope for the future.

To live, we must not at any moment lose hope. We must make every effort to achieve our hopes. When you are about to lose your hope, the most important thing is to know wholeheartedly that your hope has not left you; it is only that you are beginning to abandon hope.

Continuing to envision your own future success – clenching your teeth and saying to yourself, 'Just wait and see' – can be important. Because of your feelings of jealousy and envy, vexation, frustration, regret, and your aversion to defeat, you can grow. These feelings can be the motivating power for individual development. If you constantly envision and portray your bright future, some day that future image of yourself will indeed approach you in reality.

Hope will always be fulfilled. As long as you don't give up that hope and don't discard it, it will always become reality. Hope will present itself when it is unexpected. It absolutely will.

By continuing to hope, people are able to protect themselves from poison and illness, allowing immunity to work efficiently. Never give up in anything. The moment you give up, everything crumbles.

If you cannot envision yourself in a hopeful and shining future, it is the same as admitting that you cannot progress even one step further from where you are now. No matter how poor you are spiritually, physically, or economically, it's still very important for you to envision your bright future.

If you envision a miserable future, it will take shape through the power of the subconscious. Instead, though it may be difficult, envision your happy future surrounded by people. If you hope for this future day after day, eventually it will come. It definitely will come.

DIVINE SELF AND DIVINE MISSIONS

You need no striking talent. There is absolutely no need for you to draw people's attention to any of your talents. Instead, stand firmly on the ground and develop as a human being who finds the greatest joy in revealing your true divine Self step by step – this is the most worthy thing to do. Your rival is not others. It is you yourself.

The human heart is indeed strange. In every human heart, a stern conscience resides. Therefore, to escape from our guilty conscience – from the conflict that arises from neglected duty, effort, or patience – we justify ourselves as much as possible and try to lighten our guilt. As a result, we deceive ourselves by trying hard to convince ourselves that it was better that way or that there was no other way. With such unconscious defenses, we protect ourselves from our own guilty conscience to the maximum. For this reason, we lose sight of what lies in the innermost recesses of our hearts, our true divine Self. If we continue to deceive our own hearts and justify ourselves, a great upheaval will occur to purge such thoughts, which mask the true divine Self.

Those with immature minds and spirits try to blame others for what they themselves are responsible for. They vehemently defend themselves. They don't attempt to face things directly; instead, they attempt to run away. Such people never grow. They may be perfectly mature physically, but their spirit stopped growing at twelve or thirteen years of age. When these people stop transferring their responsibility to others, they can become true adults for the first time. When they have the courage to accept the responsibility for their actions, no matter what the consequences are, then they will have the true adult spirit.

Why do you depend on others? You were betrayed because you depended on them. Don't depend on others. Depending on others leads to no solution. Even if others may give you something that appears to be a solution, the problem has, in fact, been only temporarily resolved. Don't you realize that your strength is lost in proportion to your dependence on others? If you feel like depending on others, why don't you shift direction and depend on yourself? Is it because you lack confidence in yourself? Nothing spoils human beings as much as dependence. Be a person who can rely on your true divine Self.

Be clear and plain. It's best that your mind be simple. Make your thoughts clearly understandable to everyone. When your mind is complex and intricate, even you may not know what to do. Instead of tossing opinions back and forth, thinking That's not it, or This isn't it either, cleanly discard your thoughts, your inner questions, and your ideas. Empty your mind so that you can receive fresh inspiration from your true divine Self.

No matter how violently the typhoon may rage, its eye, or center, is absolutely calm and peaceful. Your center – your true divine Self – likewise is never disturbed by any suffering, any sorrow.

You already know that this universe evolves according to a certain order. You know also that you are led by an invisible thread as you live according to the evolution of the great universe. You know that, once you deviate from the law of the universe, you will instantly come to ruin. You also know that you exist together with great nature, that you coexist and prosper in harmony with all living things. However, today more and more people are deviating from the universal law. This is because increasing numbers of people are unable to perceive spiritual or divine energy. The time will eventually come when all will perish, unless we become clearly aware of the divine power that lies within us.

There are some people who worry too much about one thing; there are others who seriously worry about trivial matters. These are the kinds of people who tend to lose out in life. Despite the fact that they're wracking their brains more than others do, they cannot achieve accordingly. Often these people lack confidence no matter what they do, and always feel insecure and anxious. Imagining what hasn't happened, they unnecessarily worry about what to do if such things should happen. These people need to learn to change their thinking immediately. Believe in your divine missions and do your best to fulfill these missions – this says everything.

In this world, usually people abide strictly by rules and morals, learn academic subjects, make efforts and persevere, acquire high intellect and knowledge, and engage in an occupation. Some enter a religious path to practice good deeds and work at this with devotion. But what is the purpose of their life? Success, honor, power, wealth, or happiness?

As long as people's minds have a strong interest in these things, this world cannot avoid being split in two – happiness versus unhappiness, success versus failure, the rich versus the poor, health versus illness, peace versus war. The divine missions of human beings lie in expressing a way of life through existence that is beyond this kind of dichotomy. It is expressed by way of virtue. There is no longer anything to be learned in this world of dichotomy. The

rules and laws of this world exist for
humans to judge other humans. However, if
we transcend the level of rules and laws and
live in freedom, love, and forgiveness – then
we have fulfilled our divine missions.

Why do only human beings live in constant
worry? Animals and plants don't worry at all.
We never see a dog striving to be a lion; we never hear
about a chrysanthemum impatient to become a rose.
All things in the natural world live to accomplish the
missions that are given to them and live in full
contentment with what they are.

Only humans furiously try to be other than themselves.
Totally unaware that they have wonderful qualities that
cannot be found elsewhere, human beings always focus
their eyes on others, envy them, and impatiently try to
be someone else. God does not give the same thing to
everyone. God gives each person something that can be

brought to fruition only by that person. Gaze into your own inner being, and try to accomplish your divine missions. Then you will have no troubles.

You have been brought to this world with some missions, given by God. Like many others, however, you may live without purpose, not knowing what your missions are. Don't forget that the circumstances in which you are placed are your precious mission at this moment. It may be a small mission that may seem trite to you. However, by accumulating small missions, you reach a big mission. Never neglect or underestimate the value of any circumstances.

To bring to life, to the greatest possible extent, those characteristics, abilities, and talents bestowed on you by God is to accomplish your own divine missions. Potential ability in human beings differs from person to person. You must make efforts to discover yourself and thoroughly pursue your own way. Copying others – which leads to losing yourself – is your greatest enemy.

You were brought to this world for no other purpose than to build happiness, harmony, and peace for many other people.

Nothing is as foolish as predetermining that you can't do it, you're no good, it's above your ability – even before attempting to do it. If you prejudge everything in your mind, you can never advance or improve even one step, nor can you become a bigger person. Experience is the only assignment for human growth. Because you lack experience, you hesitate, get confused, and make decisions in terms of your limited scope. All you need to do is take a step forward to gain a new experience. Jump forward. A path is already there. The path is open.

———

There are only two things you must do in this lifetime: Be of service to others as much as possible, and polish your inner being to its fullest radiance.

———

ABOUT THE AUTHOR

'Behave arrogantly before no one, show anger to no one, scold no one, restrict no one, resent no one, badmouth no one, hate no one, sadden no one, criticize no one, hurt no one, discriminate against no one, betray no one, be jealous of no one, forgive everyone – this is how we should always hope to be.'

If you agree that this is the way you'd like to live – and have the rest of the world live – then you'll respond to the messages in *The Golden Key to Happiness*, a book of spiritual guidance and inspiration by a woman who has dedicated her life to world peace.

Masami Saionji is the leader of the World Peace Prayer Movement, initiated by her adoptive father, Masahisa Goi, in 1955. She is Chairperson of two peace organizations: the World Peace Prayer Society, headquartered in New York, and the Byakko Shinko Kai, founded in Japan.

Descended from the Royal Ryuku Family of Okinawa, Ms Saionji was educated in the United States as well as Tokyo. She attended Michigan State and Stanford Universities. She and her husband, a prime minister's great-grandson, have three daughters.

For three years Ms Saionji wrote a column, 'Daily Guidance,' for a Japanese magazine. *The Golden Key to Happiness* grew out of those columns. Her previous books have been published in Japan.